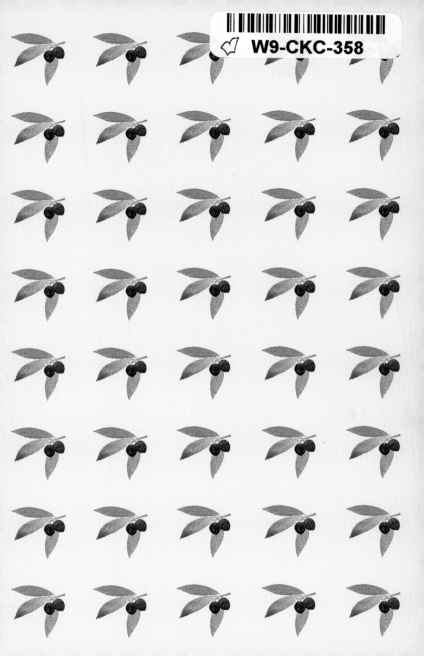

W9-CKC-358

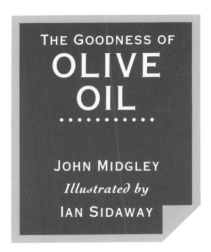

THE GOODNESS OF
OLIVE OIL
. . . .

JOHN MIDGLEY

Illustrated by

IAN SIDAWAY

RANDOM HOUSE
NEW YORK

ACKNOWLEDGEMENTS

The author thanks the following individuals for their advice and for kindly checking sections of the text: Dudley Bennett, MD, Charles Carey, Nicky Giorgio, Sue Midgley, Jo Swinnerton; The Oil Merchant for supplying olive oil for the illustrations; Antonio Carluccio and Alan Davidson for their permission to relay a recipe and an anecdote.

FURTHER READING

El Libro del Aceite y de la Aceituna, by Lourdes March and Alicia Ríos (Alianza, Madrid) is *the* bible on the subject and a source of some of the information in this book, especially on oil extraction.
Also useful is *Oils, Vinegars and Seasonings,* by Mark Lake and Judy Ridgway (Mitchell Beazley). Patience Gray's *Honey from a Weed* (Prospect Books) and *A Kitchen in Corfu,* by James Chatto and Wendy Martin (Weidenfeld & Nicolson) give tantalizing insights into the lives of olive growers.

Copyright © 1992 by John Midgley
Illustrations copyright © 1992 by Ian Sidaway

All rights reserved under International and Pan-American Copyright Conventions.

Published in the United States by Random House, Inc., New York.

This work was originally published in Great Britain by Pavilion Books Limited, London.

Library of Congress Cataloging-in-Publication Data

Midgley, John.
The goodness of olive oil/John Midgley; illustrated by Ian Sidaway.
p. cm. – (The Goodness of)
ISBN 0-679-41627-7
1. Cookery (Olive oil) 2. Olive oil. 3. Olive oil – Health aspects. I. Title. II. Series: Midgley, John. Goodness of.
TX819.042M54 1992
641.6'463 – dc20 92-13767

Manufactured in Belgium

2 4 6 8 9 7 5 3

Contents
· · · · · · · · · ·

PART
ONE
· · · · · · · · · · ·

OLIVE OIL AND HEALTH

Although olive oil has been a staple food in the Mediterranean for thousands of years, it is only relatively recently that its goodness has come under medical scrutiny, to emerge with flying colours.

Olive oil is the principal dietary fat throughout most of the region, as far as the northern margins of the cultivation of the olive tree *Olea Europea*, where it is gradually replaced by solid animal fats such as butter, lard and goose fat. To the east, in Asia Minor, in parts of the Middle East, and into Asia, it is replaced by sesame and other nut and seed oils, and ghee (clarified butter), and to the south, in the African hinterland, by peanut, coconut and palm oils.

In the West, the culinary use of olive oil is now commonplace but its widespread availability is a fairly recent phenomenon. Although olive oil of acceptable quality is generally available in the large supermarkets and multiple stores at very reasonable prices, thanks to volume buying, specialist food stores and delicatessens stock a better range of extra virgin and blended oils from different countries, predominantly Italy, Spain and Greece.

Many health-conscious cooks now use olive oil almost to the exclusion of all other cooking fats, but it is important to recognize that processed, convenience and junk foods are a rich source of animal fat. Fat itself is not bad for you, but is an essential component of a healthy diet; it is the kind of fat you consume that matters. Fats can be mainly saturated, as animal fats and their derivatives are, polyunsaturated, like grape seed, sunflower, safflower and corn oils, and monounsaturated, or they can be a combination. Doctors are increasingly recommending a reduction in our consumption of animal fats in favour of unsaturated vegetable fats and the oils present in some fish. Olive oil is low in saturated and polyunsaturated fats but very high in monounsaturates and there is now a wealth of evidence to support its alleged beneficial effects which would appear to suggest that we should consume a lot more of it.

Heart and arterial disease

It is known that eating cholesterol-rich foods and saturated (animal) fats raises blood cholesterol and that a high level of cholesterol in the blood over a long period increases the risk of cardiovascular disease. Fatty deposits of cholesterol called *plaque* build up slowly in the smooth lining of the blood vessels, narrowing their bore, roughening and hardening them (*atherosclerosis*), and so forcing the blood to flow at higher pressure, much as a gardener can increase the water pressure of a hose pipe by partially covering the hole with the thumb. Sometimes blood clots (*thromboses*) form where the blood comes into contact with these damaged surfaces of the vessel walls (*atheromas*), either blocking the vessel locally or breaking off and occluding a vessel downstream. A *coronary thrombosis* is a life-threatening condition in which the blockage of a coronary artery leads to the death of part of the heart muscle through starvation of oxygen-bearing blood to its tissue, an event known as a *coronary infarction*, or, in the vernacular, a heart attack. A thrombosis in the vessels supplying blood to the brain often results in a stroke, again through tissue death. Otherwise, sustained high blood pressure itself can lead to stroke and to kidney damage. Therefore, consumption of too much saturated fat is one factor which can lead to cardio vascular disease, as is chronic high blood pressure exacerbated by smoking, obesity and lack of exercise.

The link between dietary fat and health was established in comparative studies that were made of the effects of different national and regional diets on

disease incidence: those societies that consume a lot of cholesterol and saturated fats, (such as Britain, parts of Scandinavia and the USA) show a high incidence of heart disease, while those with low levels of saturated fats in the diet and high levels of mono- and polyunsaturated fats (Southern Italy, Greece and other countries that produce and consume olive oil) have some of the lowest incidence in the world, as do certain regions with a diet rich in fish oils. It would appear that consumption of olive oil, which is very high in monounsaturated fat, actually reduces blood cholesterol. But it is not as simple as that, because one form of blood cholesterol ('high density lipoprotein') is thought to help clear away plaque and atheromas, whereas 'low density lipoprotein' cholesterol has the opposite, damaging effect of promoting them. While polyunsaturated fats in other vegetable oils such as safflower, sunflower and grape seed do generally reduce both types of cholesterol in the blood, only fats high in monounsaturates, such as olive oil, lower the harmful kind of cholesterol while stimulating the beneficial kind, an extraordinary miracle of targetting with thousands of years of intuitive experience behind it. There is also evidence that olive oil acts as an anti-coagulant, thinning the blood in the same way that aspirin does, and this is proving to be an important therapy in the treatment of patients who have survived a heart attack.

Other benefits to health

Olive oil is also considered good for the stomach, as it can have a soothing effect on ulcers, is an aid to digestion, acts as a mild laxative, and there is some evidence that its monounsaturated fats may also be beneficial in the diet of diabetics. Some new research has revealed a link between saturated fats and the painful inflammation experienced by patients suffering from rheumatoid arthritis; a diet low in saturated fats and rich in olive oil and the fat present in oily fish such as salmon, herrings and mackerel has been recommended by some doctors as a way of reducing inflammation and pain. With its antioxidants, olive oil may also help to prevent certain cancers. There are also innumerable traditional popular remedies involving olive oil which local people swear by, for a variety of common ailments including bowel disorders, constipation, baldness, dry or chapped skin, rheumatism and sore muscles, and earache. It is believed also to encourage shiny hair and moister skin.

There are too many non-culinary uses of olive oil to discuss fully here. However, as a further tribute to this miraculous substance it is worth mentioning just a few of the many other uses for olive oil that have been found through the centuries. Olive oil has been used as an ointment since time immemorial, and its continuing religious use today in anointing the baptized, the ordained and the dying has roots that can be traced all the way back to the earliest books of the Old Testament. Indeed, legend has it that when Adam knew he was close to death, he reminded the Lord of His promise of the Oil of Forgiveness. An angel placed three seeds on his lips and after his burial, these germinated and grew into a cedar, a cypress and an olive tree. Olive oil is still used to light both roadside shrines and remote chapels in Greece and has had a long usage as lamp fuel. (The shape of Aladdin's magic lamp, so familiar from children's picture books, matches the design of oil lamps in widespread use in the Near East at that time.)

Olive oil has a classical pedigree as a hair tonic and a skin balm and is still widely used to make excellent, creamy and very natural soaps. These can even be made at home by boiling up olive oil with resin, caustic soda and water. Olive oil is also used in furniture restoration as a cleansing agent and stain-remover.

Etymology

There are two distinct roots of the words 'olive' and 'oil' which reveal their geographical origin and dissemination. On the one hand, our word 'oil' can be traced as far back as Cretan *elaiwa* and Semitic *ulu*, becoming *oleum* in Latin and *oli* in Romance languages. On the other hand, the Spanish word for oil, *aceite*, has a separate root in the Hebrew *zait*, which became *zaitum* in Arabic: *az-Zait*, to the Moorish invaders of Spain meant 'juice of the olive'. Both roots reflect the spread of the olive from east to west, coinciding with the expansion of trade, culture and civilization along the European and African shores of the Mediterranean.

The ancient world

Olive oil has been the traditional fat of the Mediterranean for at least 4000 years, possibly as many as 6000. Alongside wheat and the vine, it has been one of the three staples of Mediterranean societies for as long as communities have lived settled – as opposed to nomadic, hunter-gathering – existences. It is thought to have been cultivated first as a result of breeding experiments with the native thorny wild olive, perhaps in Persia, or in the Phoenician Levant in what are today Syria and Lebanon, and was well known by the ancient Egyptians. All the major civilizations of the Mediterranean have played a part in the dissemination of the olive throughout the region: Egyptians, Phoenicians (who were probably responsible for its introduction into Iberia, as the place name *Córdoba*, derived from the Phoenician word for olive press, *corteb*, would suggest), Cretans, Greeks, Carthaginians, Romans and Arabs.

While cultivation of the tree was spreading, economic trade between nations promoted the planting of more trees. Olive oil came to assume enormous importance in Rome and was a factor that motivated warring and subjugated nations to embrace peace. On the one hand, Rome needed to import large supplies of oil and wheat from its colonies to feed its citizens, and the oil was also in great demand as an ointment, to be used by citizens at the baths and by athletes at the games. On the other hand, the colonized nations saw that their peace, prosperity and stability lay in meeting this demand. That the olive branch is an ancient symbol of peace is not very surprising. As it takes between five and ten years after planting for the tree to bear adequate fruit, a peaceful co-existence was vital to ensure a return on the grower's investment and a continuous supply of oil.

In a second westerly expansion, this time to the New World, the Iberian conquistadors established the olive in the Caribbean, Mexico, Peru, Chile, Argentina, Brazil and California, where it flourishes in the favourable climate. The tree grows anywhere in the world where there is a Mediterranean climate, including South Africa and parts of Australia.

Olive Oil Production

Cultivation and climate

The countries bordering the Mediterranean sea produce most of the world's olives, nearly all of which are crushed for oil, and the rest – about 10 per cent – are preserved for eating. These countries possess an estimated 800 million trees, with 500 million in the European Community. The leading producer is Spain, followed closely by Italy, then Greece and Tunisia. The leading consumers per head of population are, in descending order, the Greeks (especially the Cretans), the Spaniards and Italians, the Libyans, the Syrians, the Portuguese, the Turks, the Tunisians and the French.

The olive tree will tolerate poor, rocky soil and so thrives in mountainous parts of Spain, Italy and Greece which are otherwise unsuitable for crop planting, even though it yields more fruit in undulating or lowland sites. It will not tolerate frosts below −7°C (18°F), prolonged cold weather or excessively high annual rainfall but needs a stable cycle of hot, dry summers, short, wet springs and autumns and mild winters, with plenty of sunshine throughout the year. It will, however, withstand the high winds often experienced in this part of the world. When trees are apparently killed by cold, as happened in Tuscany in 1985, the base and roots will throw up fresh shoots, but it will be some years before these are mature enough to flower and fruit. The mean annual temperature range for olive cultivation is 16–23°C (61–74°F).

Harvesting

Olive trees flower at the end of the winter and in the spring and the fruit develops very slowly, turning from green to pink and purple and finally to black when fully ripe. The tree produces flowers and fruit on the previous year's wood, and a good year tends to be followed by a less fruitful one. Black olives are usually harvested from November until February or March, while green olives are picked earlier, beginning in October. There is considerable variation in the times and techniques of harvesting. Growers in some countries allow the olives to fall of their own accord on to nets or on to cleared, prepared ground, while others beat or shake the fruit off the branches, with sticks and poles, rakes or mechanical shakers, or climb up ladders to pick them by hand before they are ripe enough to fall spontaneously. Whatever the method, it is usually exhausting and tedious work, undertaken in inclement weather, but it does bring communities together to perpetuate an unbroken chain linking them with their earliest ancestors.

The percentage of oil in the olive increases with ripeness, and oil pressed from ripe olives is golden, while less ripe olives tend to produce more peppery, pungent oils with a pronounced green colour. There are scores of different varieties – Spain alone has twenty-two – of which some of the most famous eating varieties are the Greek Kalamata, the Spanish Manzanilla (also very successfully cultivated in California) and the Italian early fruiting Ascolona which also yields very good oil. The age of the tree and the variety determine the yield. Immature trees up to twenty years old will produce far less than trees in their prime, with an age of thirty to over 100 years. Really ancient trees, over 150 years old, also yield little and have begun their slow decline into death, although some trees attain a great age of some 200 years.

Oil extraction

Olives are pressed in a variety of ways, using either methods that have barely changed over millennia, or right up-to-date technology. Small communal mills in remote villages will press an individual's sackful of olives from a handful of privately owned trees, together with everyone else's, while, at the other end of the scale, the large industrial producers press vast quantities with optimum efficiency, using the latest stainless steel mills and centrifuges. At one time even the smallest hamlets and villages had their own stone mills of an ancient design directly descended from man- or horse-driven Greek and Roman prototypes. In some Greek tavernas you may stumble across a vast, circular stone receptacle where once olives were crushed, more likely than not in current service as a storage bin for beer and Coca-Cola bottles. Ancient or modern, the process of oil extraction is essentially a simple one, involving up to five main stages: washing; crushing; grinding; pressing; and decanting or other-wise separating the oil from the water.

First the olives are brought in and laid out, usually in an outdoor receiving area where they can be checked for condition and sorted according to their maturation, which will influence the acidity level of the ensuing oil. Any leaves and twigs still adhering to them will be removed, either manually or with industrial blowers.

As olives must be processed very soon after delivery to the mill, before fermentation sets in, milling is often started only a few hours later, and certainly within two or three days: this short delay is thought to assist oil extraction by conditioning the olives. Next, the olives are washed in cold water, then drained, before being crushed to break up the tissues and release the oil. This can be done by traditional methods, with mechanical rollers, or in modern, stainless steel crushers which work by simultaneously cutting, shearing and rubbing. (This method is extremely quick and efficient but tiny metal particles do get into the oil.) Then they are ground into a smooth paste, stones (pits) and all, the purpose of which is to concentrate the small droplets released on crushing into larger drops of oil, while generating heat to encourage the oil to flow freely. (The stones harbour a lot of oil.) Traditionally, the paste is now spread out on to natural fibre mats which will be stacked layer upon layer in a vertical press to extract, with relatively little pressure, what is known as the first cold pressing of oil. Alternatively the oil can be extracted in a continuous centrifuge.

If a modern centrifuge is used for oil extraction, the paste produced by milling and crushing is fed into the machine, which spins at high velocity to separate the oil from the pulp. The oil emerging from press or centrifuge is actually a reddish mixture of oil, vegetable matter and water. This can be decanted manually or put into another centrifuge to separate the oil from the water.

The cloudy, unfiltered oil is then stored in large containers. The ratio of olives to oil is approximately five kilos of fruit to each litre of oil. This oil can be filtered, to remove the sediment, or, more primitively, left to rest so that the sediment can naturally fall with gravity to accumulate at the bottom of the storage containers as the temperature rises in the spring and the oil becomes less viscous.

Either way, this is 'virgin' olive oil. 'Pure' olive oil is made by blending oil of originally high acidity, from second or subsequent pressings which are then subjected to a process of refinement, with first-pressed, virgin oils. In the European Community the term 'pure olive oil', as just defined, was recently changed simply to 'olive oil'. To be labelled 'extra virgin', oil must have an acidity of 0.2–1 per cent. 'Olive oil' should not exceed 1.5 per cent of acidity. (The higher the acidity, the poorer the quality, leading eventually to a certain toxicity.) Other processes involving hot-water pressings of the residue cakes and use of solvents produce oil for industrial use and soap-making. The oily vegetable waste can be burned as fuel, converted to fertilizer and treated for use as cattle feed.

1ʳᵉ Qualite **COMESTIBLE**

Choosing oil

U nfortunately, the best extra virgin olive oils are
very expensive. It is an expense that no serious
cook should avoid, but when paying out a king's
ransom for a litre of liquid gold, take consolation from
the certainty of the pleasures that await you and the
comforting knowledge that premium oil of this quality
will stretch a very long way and should not be wasted
on frying, but kept to enrich raw or prepared dishes.
And there *are* far more expensive flavourings, such as
aged balsamic vinegar, so take heart!

In general, extra virgin oil with its rich, fruity
flavour is best when you want the food to taste
superbly of olives, especially in uncooked dishes, and
to dress salads, soups, vegetables and cold meats.
Lighter, refined oils are perfect for frying or for
making more delicate dishes such as mayonnaise
which the obtrusive flavour of extra virgin oil would
overwhelm. The recipes will each prescribe whether
'extra virgin' or (refined) 'olive oil' are called for.

The colour, nose and taste of olive oil are
conditioned by many different factors: the ripeness of
the fruit on harvesting, the climate and soil, the

hundreds of olive varieties, and so on. However, one might hazard a sweeping generalization in so far as most Tuscan extra virgin oils tend to be thick, green and smell and taste fruity, sometimes distinctly peppery, while the extra virgin olive oils of Southern Italy (Puglia, Calabria, Liguria and Sicily are the most productive regions), tend to be a paler greeny-gold, but strong to taste and smell. Of the high-quality single-estate Italian extra virgin oils, connoisseurs value particularly the *Colonna, Tenuta Caparzo* and *Saragano* brands and the famous oil marketed by the Chianti estate of *Badia a Coltibuono*. An excellent example of an unfiltered, farmhouse extra virgin oil is made on an estate near Florence and marketed under the label of *Dell' Ugo*. This has a robust peppery taste and a wonderfully natural cloudy, green colour. These are all premium quality uncommercial oils equivalent to the *grands crus* wines, but if you cannot obtain them, there are many other good commercial extra virgin oils, including the well-known brands *Berio, Sasso, Menucci* and *de Cecco*.

Although ranked low on the world's production tables, the olive oils of Provence are esteemed and widely available. Although mostly golden or yellow in colour, some of the finest extra virgin oils are distinctly green, including those that are produced in the Valley of Les Baux, and the commended *Le Vieux Moulin* label from Nyons. These and oils from neighbouring Nîmes are widely acknowledged to be the best in France. Good quality commercially made blends of Provençal oils that you are likely to encounter include the brand names *Plagniol* and *A l'Olivier*, which has a marvellous specialist shop in Paris. A visit to the *Alziari* shop at 14 Rue St. François de Paul is recommended to any oleophile who may be passing through Nice.

Spain vies with Italy as the world's largest producer, and this is where my favourite everyday, mass-produced oils come from. On the infamous

occasions when adulterated oils tragically have poisoned many hundreds of unsuspecting people, these have always been traced to cheap oil tainted with industrial compounds unfit for human consumption, sold door-to-door in unmarked containers by unscrupulous travelling vendors. In fact, the record of the leading commercial brands, including *Carbonell* and *Ybarra*, is impeccable and you need have no worries about buying any of the Spanish olive oil you will find on sale. Lérida in north-east Spain is considered the finest oil-producing region, with delicate, straw-coloured oils which have gained quite a following amongst the cognoscenti. The *Lérida* brand, shown on the cover, is an extra virgin olive oil made exclusively from the Arbequina olive, which has won several medals and accolades of late. But Spain's largest and most productive provinces are Jaén, Córdoba, Málaga and Granada, all in Andalucía, and it is mostly these oils that go into the blends of the household brands.

Greek olive oil is generally of good quality and represents particularly excellent value for money. On Corfu and in other traditional Greek rural communities, the family olive trees are still both master and servant, compelling many back-breaking hours of toil collecting the fallen olives from a ground that has been draped with black nylon nets. The olives are usually sent away to be crushed in a communal mill. The ensuing oil will be used not only for cooking, but also for anointing babies at baptisms, mixed with lime to produce domestic whitewash, poured into uncorked wine bottles to seal the remaining wine from contact with the air, and poured over shallow waters to reveal with gin-like clarity the whereabouts of shoals of fish, squid and octopus. Left-over oil from cooking will be discreetly collected by the representative of a leading cosmetics company, to make soap. With so many applications, no wonder these canny country folk have chosen not to sacrifice their precious olive groves on the altar of tourist development and hotel construction. Greece is the world's third largest producer of olive oil and one of the largest consumers, with a staggering per capita consumption of 25 litres a year. Cultivation is intensive, albeit on a reduced scale, based at many small farms, co-operatives and small holdings, in complete contrast with Spain's vast tracts of terrain planted with olives, owned by the large commercial manufacturers. Koroneiki olives grown on the Mani peninsula produce the finest extra virgin olive oil in Greece.

Portugal, Turkey, Morocco, Tunisia, Algeria, Libya, Syria, Jordan and the Lebanon also produce good quality olive oil, employing traditional methods, and other, more marginal producers include Egypt, Iran, Yugoslavia, Albania, Israel, Peru, Chile, Brazil, Argentina, Mexico and California.

Tasting oils

The appreciation of quality oils has become quite a serious subject for study and has attracted the attention of food writers and critics. This has resulted not only in the adoption of an oil parlance every bit as quaint and fanciful – some would say pretentious – as that applied to wine, but also in promotional olive oil tastings. Traditionally, oil, like wine, is assessed by its appearance, smell and taste. Usually olive oils are tasted on small pieces of plain white bread, which are the perfect neutral backdrop to the taste of the oils. The colour can be verified by pouring different oils on to unpatterned white dishes. Country people and olive growers also judge the quality of olive oil by pouring a little on to the back of the hand and gently rubbing it in, then inhaling the aroma. In Italy, tasters decked out in laboratory coats are employed by the regulating authorities to check and classify oil. Their method is that of the wine taster: a swirl in the glass and a holding up to the light to check colour, another swirl, a good, deep sniff, then a mouthful.

Cooking with olive oil

Olive oil can be heated to higher temperatures before burning than nut and seed oils which are high in polyunsaturates and is thus an excellent frying medium or one in which to quickly sear meat, poultry or meaty fish, sealing in the juices. However, once the oil has really smoked, it is best not to re-use it, as potentially harmful chemical changes occur in all oils at such high temperatures. Do, however, save oil in which aromatic or pungent ingredients such as garlic or chillies have been gently simmered, as these will deliciously flavour food subsequently cooked in that oil. Never pour hot oil back into the bottle, especially if the container is plastic. Instead keep a separate glass or ceramic container handy. Olive oil can be restored to

its original clarity once filtered through paper towel and after a sprig of parsley or a piece of lettuce has been simmered in it. However, it is best not to re-use it more than twice, as the more times it is used, the more likely it is to smoke and the less effective are its nutritional benefits. To deep-fry most ingredients, especially battered, breadcrumbed or floured fish, meat or vegetables, and french fries, make sure the oil is very hot and the ingredients are completely dry and not too cold. Really hot olive oil will form a film around the food and prevent too much oil from being absorbed by it. Extra virgin oil will impart its flavour in marinades and when drizzled on to barbecued foods before they are fully cooked. One of my favourite cooking techniques is to cook meat, fish or poultry, which has rested for some time in a bath of seasoned extra virgin olive oil, on a Spanish cast-iron hot plate, or griddle, called a *plancha*.

Infusions of olive oil and herbs or spices are fun to make, decorative and taste wonderful and some suggestions are given on pages 64 and 65. For a real gourmet experience, try to find some truffle-flavoured oil: the combination of premium extra virgin olive oil and truffle must make this one of the most luxurious and expensive flavourings in existence.

With its assertive flavour and ability efficiently to displace air, olive oil is also the perfect preserving medium, and many vegetables as well as wild mushrooms and sun-dried tomatoes are traditionally sterilized with pickling spices in a weak solution of watery vinegar, before being preserved *sott'olio* (literally: 'under the oil'). Some recipes for preserving in oil are given on pages 61 to 63.

Extra virgin oil is a wonderful flavouring for all manner of foods, whether to anoint wafer-thin slices of *bresaola* (cured beef), or to add to soups, salads and vegetables. No table in Spain, Portugal, Italy, Greece or Provence would be complete without an olive oil dispenser to refract the light in a gentle pool of greenish gold.

Note to the recipes

The recipes are intended to serve four, although some will stretch to six in smaller portions, as appetizers.

PART
TWO
· · · · · · · · · ·

Pamb'oli, Pa'amb Tomaquet

(Bread, olive oil and tomato)

In most of Spain and other olive oil producing countries, butter used to be virtually absent in the diet and olive oil was the fat that was sometimes put on bread, usually with some other basic seasoning such as garlic, tomato, salt, olives or paprika, or a combination of these. A popular children's snack is a sweet version of bread-and-oil, with a sprinkling of sugar or some honey. *Pamb'oli* which translates literally as 'oily bread' is a traditional *merienda*, or snack, from the Balearic islands, the ingredients of which can be carried easily by workers to their fields, olive and almond groves and assembled for consumption on the spot. Across the water, in Catalonia, a similar snack is known as *Pa'amb tomaquet* (literally, 'bread and tomato'). With the growth of an urban middle class, the peasant's rural, open-air snack has evolved into a domestic, sedentary meal, called *la merienda*, usually taken in the late afternoon or early evening. An open air café or picnic spot is known as *merendero* and several such establishments perched high on the mountainous corniche of the north coast of Mallorca specialize in *Pamb'oli*, and with their breathtakingly vertiginous views over the sparkling Mediterranean are favourites with visitors and locals alike.

loaf of strongly flavoured crusty bread
2 cloves of garlic, peeled and crushed
2 very red, ripe and juicy tomatoes
extra virgin olive oil
4 slices of cured ham (Serrano, Parma, or Bayonne)

Slice the loaf obliquely into eight rounds, each about
3½ cm/1½ inches thick. Very lightly toast these on
both sides.

Rub them with the garlic. Wash and dry the
tomatoes, cut them in half and gently both squeeze and
rub them on to one side of all the slices of bread.
Dribble about a tablespoon of oil over one side of each
slice, then place a slice of ham on half of the slices.
Cover with the remaining slices and serve as a delicious
appetizer, or as a light lunch.

Pa'amb tomaquet is similar but without the ham, so
salt should be added.

SPAGHETTINI WITH OLIVE OIL, GARLIC AND PARSLEY

• • • • • • • • • •

This is a classic example of Southern Italian *cucina povera* (poor people's fare) which, notwithstanding the meagre store-cupboard ingredients, will pleasurably fill a hungry stomach. Traditionally, no cheese is served but enough bread to wipe away the last drop of delicious, pungent oil. Use factory-made, durum wheat pasta.

salt
a drop of oil
450g/1lb spaghettini or tagliolini
3fl oz/6 tbs fruity or extra virgin olive oil
2 cloves of. garlic, peeled and chopped
1 dried chilli pepper, crumbled
salt and freshly milled black pepper
generous handful of flat-leaved (Italian) parsley, washed and chopped

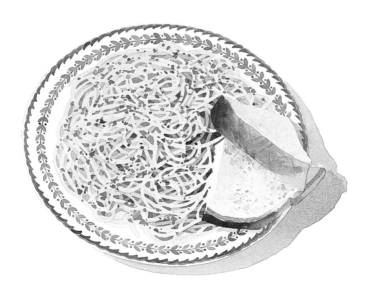

Heat plenty of water to a vigorous boil in your largest pot. Add a drop of oil and salt and, when the water returns to a fast boil, add the spaghettini. Stir well and cook about 10 minutes, until *al dente*.

Meanwhile, heat the oil in a small frying pan and add the garlic, chilli and seasoning. Simmer for a minute, then remove before the garlic burns. Throw in the parsley, which will crackle. When the pasta is ready, drain well and put it into a heated serving bowl. Quickly reheat the oil and pour over the pasta, mixing well. Serve.

SALSA VERDE

Widely prepared in a variety of ways in countries as diverse as Spain (especially in Catalonia), Italy and France, this green sauce is usually served with fish but is perhaps most closely associated with the classic Milanese meat dish, *bollito misto*. Parsley, garlic and olive oil are the essential basic ingredients, but various other herbs such as tarragon, mint and marjoram and flavouring ingredients such as capers and anchovies may be added, lemon juice used instead of vinegar, and the bread omitted.

2/3 cup fresh parsley, washed and chopped
1 clove of garlic, peeled and finely chopped
1/4 of a medium onion, very finely chopped
1 slice of bread, crumbled
2 tsp red or white wine vinegar
salt
freshly milled black pepper
110ml/4fl oz/1/2 cup extra virgin olive oil

Combine all the ingredients except the olive oil in a bowl and mix well. Stir in the olive oil and mix again.

SPAGHETTI ALLA PUTTANESCA
· · · · · · · · · ·

This very rich sauce for spaghetti is named after the Neapolitan prostitutes who supposedly invented it. The name may just as well allude to its spicy sauciness, much enhanced by the ripe olives. Factory-made durum wheat pasta is best with this sauce, and it is certainly what Neapolitans would use.

drop of olive oil
1 tsp salt
2fl oz/4 tbs extra virgin olive oil
1 dried red chilli pepper, crumbled
3 cloves of garlic, peeled and chopped
30g/1oz capers, rinsed
450g/1 lb can of tomatoes, chopped, or 4–6 ripe, fresh, plum tomatoes, peeled and chopped
1 tsp salt
freshly milled black pepper
350g/12oz factory-made spaghetti or spaghettini
12 black olives, stoned, (pitted) and roughly chopped
a few leaves of basil, washed and torn just before serving

Heat plenty of water in a very large pan, add the drop of oil and the salt and bring to a vigorous boil.

Meanwhile, prepare the sauce ingredients: heat the extra virgin oil in a frying pan large enough to accommodate the sauce and the pasta, and when just smoking, add the chilli, garlic and capers. Stir and cook for about 30 seconds, or until the garlic starts to colour. Add the chopped tomatoes, salt and pepper and mix well.

Simmer for about 5 minutes if using fresh tomatoes (20 minutes if canned).

By now the water should be boiling furiously. Add the spaghetti to the pan of boiling water and stir. This will take about 10 minutes to cook. Turn off the sauce while the spaghetti is cooking.

Drain the pasta, add the olives to the sauce and re-heat it. Toss it thoroughly with the pasta. Tear up the basil and scatter over the spaghetti. Serve with bread.

MARINADE FOR BARBECUED CHICKEN

This simple marinade is common throughout Southern Italy, the Balkans and the Middle East. Serve the chicken with barbecued summer vegetables, such as courgettes (zucchini) and sweet peppers, and a saffron *pilaf*, garnishing with lemon wedges. This may also be prepared on a hot griddle or under the grill (broiler).

1 corn-fed or free-range chicken, divided into breast and
leg portions (skin on)
225ml/8fl oz/1 cup extra virgin olive oil, or to cover
juice of a lemon
2 cloves of garlic, peeled and crushed
fresh herbs, including a bay leaf and sprigs of marjoram,
rosemary and thyme
freshly milled black pepper
salt

Put the chicken pieces in a deep bowl. Lightly beat the olive oil and lemon juice. Add the remaining ingredients, except the salt, and mix. Pour over the chicken pieces and turn them around. Marinate for at least an hour. When your barbecue is ready, remove the chicken and place on the rack, starting with the legs, which will take longer to cook. Turn once, baste with a little of the marinade and continue to cook until done. Sprinkle with salt before serving.

SOME VARIATIONS ON
THE THEME OF PESTO
· · · · · · · · · ·

Pesto, the aromatic sauce from Liguria made to flavour pasta, soups and vegetables, is now so well known and loved that it would be unnecessary to repeat the recipe here in full. (It is essentially garlic, fresh basil, olive oil, pine nuts and parmesan and/or pecorino cheese, pounded together in a pestle and mortar). However, with a little ingenuity and experimentation, you can modify the classic version by substituting different ingredients, with equally delicious results. These variations on pesto work just as well as a sauce for pasta as they do served with barbecued lamb, chicken or meaty steaks of tuna or swordfish, as a relish.

Walnut pesto

12 walnuts
1 clove of garlic, peeled
salt
handful of parsley, washed
handful of basil, washed
2 or 3 sprigs of fresh mint, washed
225ml/8fl oz/1 cup extra virgin olive oil
freshly milled black pepper

Tap the pointed ends of the walnuts with a hammer or wooden mallet to break the shells. Remove the meats from the shells and put them in a sturdy pestle and mortar or into the bowl of a food processor.

Crush the garlic with some salt and add to the walnuts. Start pounding, if using a pestle and mortar. Add the herbs and pound again (or add them to the food processor).

Start adding the oil in a thin trickle, pounding all the while (if processing, pour in the oil with the motor running.) Pound away or process until you have a smooth, quite runny and very aromatic green sauce. Season with black pepper. Note the absence of cheese.

Sun-dried tomato pesto

8 sun-dried tomato halves
(soaked in water, or from a jar, in oil)
2fl oz/4 tbs olive oil if using tomatoes already in oil in a jar
(add a little more oil if using dry tomatoes)
2 cloves of garlic, peeled
salt
6 leaves of basil, washed
2 small dried or fresh chillies

If using dry tomatoes, soak them first in a little water for an hour to soften them. Put everything in the bowl of a food processor and process thoroughly. Transfer to a bowl and serve as a relish (a little goes a long way).

GREEN OLIVE PASTES

Pastes of green olives can be bought or, better still, made at home. The first version is intended as a sauce for pasta, the second to spread on bread or pizzas.

For the pasta sauce, the quantities will produce approximately 350g/12oz of paste, enough for 4–6 servings. Just work the paste into the drained pasta while it is still very hot and serve with parmesan, freshly grated off the block, bread and a seasonal salad. The milk will eventually turn, so this sauce should be kept in the fridge for no longer than 24 hours.

225g/½lb stoned (pitted) green olives
1 tsp fennel seeds
1 clove of garlic, peeled
freshly milled black pepper
2fl oz/4 tbs extra virgin olive oil
1fl oz/2 tbs milk

Work all the ingredients in a food processor until you have a smooth paste.

An altogether different paste can be made by combining the same quantity of green olives and extra virgin olive oil with 2 peeled cloves of garlic and a generous handful of fresh basil and processing them to a coarse paste.

TAPENADE

Named after the Provençal word for caper, *tapéno* (*taper* in Catalan), *tapenade* is usually served on bread or toast, but a small quantity added to hot pasta is delicious. *Tapenade* will keep well in the fridge for a week or so. You can vary the proportions of the ingredients and add mustard and tuna fish. This version is neither overwhelmingly powerful nor in any way bland.

170g/6oz small black olives, preferably the shrivelled
Provençal varieties (30–40, depending on size)
2 anchovy fillets from a can
1 clove of garlic, peeled
3 tbs capers, rinsed
pinch of thyme or oregano
2 tsp brandy
1 tbs lemon juice
freshly milled black pepper
3fl oz/6 tbs extra virgin olive oil

If the olives are whole, cut away as much flesh as you can. Put them in a food processor with the other ingredients, except the olive oil, and blend for a minute. Now slowly add the oil in a stream and process until you have a smooth paste. To keep, cover with a thin layer of olive oil.

MARINATED STRIPS OF VEAL OR BEEF WITH GREEN OLIVES AND MUSHROOMS

T he very Italian ingredients are treated here in an oriental way, rapidly fried after a period of marination to flavour the meat, and are enhanced by the bacon, mushrooms and olives. Serve with a vegetable purée: potatoes (see page 55), cannelini beans or celeriac (celery root), dressed with olive oil, of course. Also good with this dish are fennel bulbs braised in olive oil, with parmesan.

1kg/2¼lb veal escalopes, or beef tenderloin, or rump
225ml/8fl oz/1 cup olive oil
1 onion, peeled and roughly chopped
2 cloves of garlic, peeled
1fl oz/2 tbs dry sherry or dry vermouth
freshly milled black pepper
3 slices of bacon
110g/4oz shiitake, oyster or button mushrooms, chopped
140ml/5fl oz/2/3 cup dry white wine
salt
16 stoned (pitted) green olives

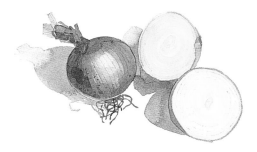

Slice the veal or beef into strips 2cm/1 inch wide, ½cm/¼ inch thick and put them into a bowl.

Prepare the marinade by adding two-thirds of the olive oil, half the chopped onion, 1 chopped clove of garlic, the sherry or vermouth, and black pepper. Mix well, cover and leave for at least one hour, preferably longer.

Finely chop the other garlic clove. Trim the bacon and cut it into small strips. Heat a heavy frying pan and add the remaining olive oil then add the bacon, remaining onion and garlic and sauté until soft, without burning. Add the mushrooms and mix well.

Meanwhile, heat a smaller non-stick frying pan, then rapidly seal the meat in the oil that will still cling to it from the marinade. Do this in batches so as not to overcrowd the pan. When the meat has all been sealed, transfer it to the pan containing the mushrooms. Deglaze the other pan with the wine, loosening any scraps. When bubbling, pour the winey juices over the main ingredients and continue to cook until the sauce is thick and the wine has all but evaporated, about 3 minutes more. Season. Add the olives and heat through. Transfer to a heated serving dish, the meat to one side and the purée or braised fennel bulbs to the other.

SWORDFISH KEBABS

In the eastern Mediterranean where swordfish are caught in large numbers, they are cooked in a mouthwatering variety of ways. Alan Davidson recounts in his book *Seafood* a curious practice first recorded by an 18th century traveller whereby Sicilian fishermen would soothe swordfish basking near the water's surface by uttering a few words of Greek, lest the brutes should dive out of their harpoons' reach on hearing Italian voices – presumably because Sicilians were so much more adept than Greeks at catching them. This simple Cypriot recipe undoubtedly works best with a wood or charcoal barbecue but is none the less suitable for an ordinary domestic grill (broiler).

1 kg/2¼ lb swordfish steaks, cut into 2cm/1 inch cubes
juice of 2 lemons and 4 lemon wedges, to garnish
225ml/8fl oz/1 cup olive oil
4 green peppers, roughly chopped into 2cm/1 inch squares
1 large aubergine (eggplant), in 1cm/½ inch wedges
3 large onions, peeled and quartered
4 firm tomatoes, quartered
4 spring onions (scallions), thinly sliced
handful of fresh parsley, washed and chopped
salt
freshly milled black pepper

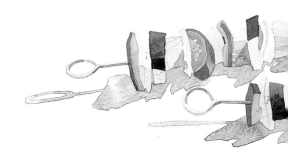

Put the swordfish in a bowl with half of the lemon juice, olive oil and seasoning, to marinate for an hour. Mix the remaining olive oil and lemon juice in a cup. Thread squares of green pepper, chunks of swordfish, aubergine wedges, pieces of onion, more swordfish and tomato on to skewers, repeating until the ingredients are used up. Barbecue over white-hot charcoal or wood embers, turning occasionally and basting with a little of the remaining olive oil and lemon juice (reserving some), until done, about 15 minutes. To serve, pour the remaining olive oil and lemon juice over the skewers and sprinkle with the spring onion and parsley and a little more salt and black pepper. Garnish with the lemon wedges and serve with rice or french fries or some good bread and a salad.

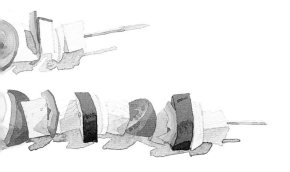

MELITZANOSALATA
· · · · · · · · · ·

This delicious *meze* of puréed aubergine (eggplant), garlic and olive oil is found all over Greece.

2 medium or 450g/1lb aubergines (eggplants)
2 cloves of garlic, peeled and finely chopped
1 tbs Greek yoghurt
1fl oz/2tbs lemon juice
3fl oz/6 tbs olive oil
1 tsp salt
pinch of cayenne or paprika
chopped flesh of 6 black olives
handful of fresh parsley, washed and chopped

Heat the oven to 220°C/425°F/gas mark 7. Wash and dry the aubergines, put them on a sheet of aluminium foil and bake until soft, about 45 minutes.

When they are cool enough to touch, slice them in half and scoop out all their flesh. Process in a food processor to a smooth paste with the other ingredients except the parsley and olive pieces. Garnish with the olives and parsley and serve with bread, or *crudités*.

MAYONNAISE

Supposedly originating in the Menorcan port of Mahon, mayonnaise (Mahon-esa) is the most widely used emulsified sauce, with many variations of colour and flavourings, including a version made with green herbs and the fiery orange *rouille*, made with garlic and served with fish soups. Although traditionally whisked by hand, it lends itself perfectly to the food processor. If the eggs are straight out of the fridge, the emulsion will probably separate, so always ensure that the ingredients are at room temperature. It is also important to add the olive oil (extra virgin is unsuitable) in a thin trickle at first. Your mayonnaise will keep in the fridge for a few days if stored in an airtight container.

2 egg yolks
1fl oz/2 tbs lemon juice
1 tsp salt
½ tsp mild mustard
225ml/8fl oz/1 cup olive oil

Put the egg yolks, lemon juice, salt and mustard in a food processor and blend. With the motor running, add a steady, thin stream of olive oil and gradually increase the flow as the sauce thickens, stopping when it is thick and glossy.

Rabbit or Chicken alla Cacciatora

Alla cacciatora means 'hunter's style', presumably because herbs, wild mushrooms and game were all available to hunters roaming the fields and woods.

700g/1½lb rabbit or chicken pieces
12g/½oz dried porcini (cep, king boletus) mushrooms
2fl oz/4 tbs olive oil
2 sage leaves, sprig each of thyme and rosemary
2 cloves of garlic, peeled and chopped
140ml/5fl oz/⅔ cup dry white wine
3 fresh or canned plum tomatoes, peeled and chopped
salt and freshly milled black pepper
12 stoned (pitted) black olives

Clean and trim the pieces of rabbit or chicken. Soak the dried mushrooms in a cup of hot water.

Heat the olive oil in a large lidded pot and brown the pieces of rabbit or chicken, then remove them. Simmer the herbs in the hot oil for a minute, then add the garlic. When this begins to turn golden, add the wine and tomatoes and bring them to a fast boil, before returning the poultry or rabbit to the pot.

Line a strainer with paper towel and drain the mushrooms, reserving their liquid, and add both to the pot. Season, turn the heat to low, partly cover, and simmer for 25 minutes more. A minute or two before serving, transfer the rabbit or chicken to a heated serving dish, remove the herbs and add the olives to the sauce. If it is runny, increase the heat to reduce the liquid. Pour the sauce over the pieces and serve with mashed or sautéed potatoes.

Deep-Fried Stuffed Olives

Try to find the larger varieties of green olive for this snack and serve straight away.

1 tbs capers, rinsed and finely chopped
peel of ½ lemon, washed and coarsely grated or slivered
1 clove of garlic, peeled and finely chopped
small piece of stale bread, crust removed, and finely crumbled
1 tomato, peeled and finely chopped
1 tbs olive oil
handful of fresh parsley, washed and chopped
freshly milled black pepper
a little flour
225g/½lb large stoned (pitted) green olives
225ml/8fl oz/1 cup olive oil

Combine all the ingredients except the flour and green olives in a bowl and mix well. With the stem end of a teaspoon, stuff the mixture into as many green olives as the occasion demands. Roll them in flour and fry in very hot olive oil for no more than thirty seconds. Serve at once.

OLIVE PATTIES

Olives and olive oil are used frequently in baking, whether in cakes, to make country bread, or flat Italian *focaccie*, baked with herbs.

These flat Turkish patties are similar to Italian *focaccia*, but rather more moist. However, they contain no yeast and are very simple to prepare and sufficiently versatile to enjoy on their own, or you could improvise cheese, tomato and herb toppings, turning them into pizzas. They must be served hot, whether straight out of the oven or reheated.

2 eggs
225ml/8fl oz/1 cup milk
small pinch of dried oregano,
or chopped leaves of rosemary
1 tsp salt
225g/½lb/1¼ cups plain (all-purpose) flour
170g/6oz roughly chopped green olives
110ml/4fl oz/½ cup extra virgin olive oil

Preheat the oven to 180°C/350°F/gas mark 4.

Beat the eggs and milk in a mixing bowl with a whisk until frothy. Add the herbs and salt and gradually mix in the flour. Beat thoroughly to a runny paste and mix in the chopped olives and the olive oil. Spoon the mixture into a large, shallow, oiled baking tin (pan) and bake for 25 minutes until lightly browned.

CHICKEN BREASTS WITH OLIVES
· · · · · · · · · ·

This version of a North African dish involves three stages of preparation: first the browning of the chicken pieces in olive oil; then the base of onion, spices, tomatoes and water, cooked slowly until the onion melts away into the sauce; and finally, the return of the chicken breasts to finish cooking, with more onions. It is important to keep the skin on, as this prevents the chicken from drying out.

Alternatively, a whole bird can be browned in the oil, then cooked with the base, without removing it from the pot: extend the cooking time by 10 minutes.

4 corn-fed or free-range chicken breasts, skin on, or a whole, cleaned chicken
3fl oz/6 tbs of olive oil
1 medium onion, peeled, halved vertically then finely sliced
salt and freshly milled black pepper
2cm/1 inch piece of fresh ginger, peeled and finely chopped
2 tsp paprika
1 tsp cayenne
3 canned or fresh tomatoes, chopped
225ml/8fl oz/1 cup of water and a little extra
1 medium onion, peeled and finely chopped
12 black olives, stoned (pitted) and chopped
handful of fresh parsley, washed and chopped

Heat the olive oil in a deep, heavy pan and brown the chicken breasts in it. Remove them from the pan.

Add the finely sliced onion, seasoning, ginger, paprika, cayenne, tomatoes and water. Bring to the boil, then reduce to a simmer and cook, covered, for 45 minutes, stirring occasionally and checking that the sauce does not dry out. (You may have to add more water.)

Return the chicken breasts to the pan, add the finely chopped onion and a little more water if necessary to keep the sauce thick but not dry. Cover and simmer very gently for 20 minutes, basting with the sauce from time to time.

Arrange the chicken breasts on a hot serving dish or on individual plates, surrounded by a little of the dense sauce and topped with the olive pieces and parsley. Serve with rice or potatoes.

OLIVE, FENNEL AND CHERRY TOMATO SALAD

············

Olives put in an appearance in a variety of Mediterranean salads. This is an especially colourful combination with interesting flavour and texture contrasts, but other, more traditional salads are equally satisfying to the eye and palate; for example, an authentic Niçoise salad or a Greek country salad with feta cheese and black olives.

4 fennel bulbs, trimmed and outer husks removed
450g/1lb cherry tomatoes
1 large cucumber, peeled and diced
20 Kalamata olives (stones removed)
12 rocket or young spinach leaves
1½fl oz/3 tbs extra virgin olive oil
1fl oz/2 tbs of balsamic vinegar
salt

Wash and thoroughly dry the vegetables.

Slice each fennel bulb vertically two or three times and slice again to produce thin strips. Put them in a bowl and mix with the cherry tomatoes, cucumber, olives, rocket or spinach and arrange to provide an attractive combination of green, black, red and white ingredients.

Beat the olive oil with the vinegar, dress and season the salad just before serving.

An authentic *salade Niçoise* is made with quartered hard cooked eggs, sliced tomatoes, lettuce, green peppers, anchovy fillets and black olives. Sometimes cooked vegetables such as green beans and potatoes are added. Dress with extra virgin olive oil beaten with red wine vinegar, a little chopped garlic, basil and a pinch of sugar.

To make a Greek country salad, combine a few slices of onion, some shredded lettuce, green pepper rings and chunks of peeled cucumber and quartered tomatoes, with luscious Kalamata olives, topped with plenty of crumbled feta cheese. Dress only with extra virgin olive oil and a little salt, bearing in mind that the cheese is very salty.

Pepper Salad

This colourful Italian *antipasto* of scorched and peeled peppers is a celebration of summer itself and is particularly suitable for taking on a picnic, if transported in a leak-proof jar. The scorching and removal of the indigestible skins seems to sweeten the flesh. Serve with plenty of crusty bread to mop up the juices.

4–6 yellow and red peppers
1fl oz/2 tbs extra virgin olive oil
1 clove of garlic, peeled and finely chopped
white part of 2 spring onions (scallions), thinly sliced
generous handful of flat-leaved (Italian) parsley, washed and chopped
salt and freshly milled black pepper
a few drops of balsamic or good quality red wine vinegar

Scorch the peppers until the skins are black either by holding them with long tongs over a gas flame, or by grilling (broiling). Place them in a bowl, cover and leave them to cool for a quarter of an hour or so.

Now scrape off the blackened skins with a knife but do not rinse them. Slice off the tops with the stalks attached and remove the inner membranes and seeds. Slice what is left of the flesh into strips approximately 1cm/½ inch wide. Put them in an attractive serving bowl and add the olive oil, turning them around so they are well coated. Add the garlic, spring onions, parsley and seasoning and mix well. Leave for not less than 2 hours and, just before serving, sprinkle with the vinegar.

TORTILLA
. . . .

The genuine Spanish omelette is made only with potatoes, eggs, olive oil and onions. Occasionally, a little garlic may be added. It is eaten barely warm or at room temperature but never hot, and is always available as a bar snack, either in small squares (*pinchos*) or in larger triangular wedges (*raciones*), inevitably resting on bread speared with a wooden toothpick.

> 5 very fresh free-range eggs, beaten
> ½ onion, peeled and roughly chopped
> 2 medium potatoes, peeled and thinly sliced
> 2fl oz/4 tbs fruity olive oil
> salt

Heat the oil in a small, well-seasoned or non-stick frying pan. Put in the potatoes and the onion, cover, turn heat to low and simmer until the potatoes are soft, stirring to ensure the onion does not burn black but allowing it to brown and sweeten.

Meanwhile, pre-heat the grill (broiler). Season the beaten eggs and pour them into the pan. When the underside begins to brown (lift up a corner of the omelette to verify), remove the pan and put it under the grill (broiler). The top side will bubble up and foam a little. It is done when the crust develops brown spots. Remove, tip away any surplus oil and allow to cool. Serve accompanied by mayonnaise, bread, and a salad.

POTATOES MASHED WITH OLIVE OIL

I n Mediterranean kitchens, potatoes are usually mashed with a little milk and fruity olive oil, instead of butter. A vogue for Mediterranean flavours has succeeded in converting northern palates to this traditional southern European way of dressing puréed potatoes and vegetables. An old-fashioned hand-held masher works best.

water
1 tsp salt
1kg/2¼lb floury baking or all-purpose potatoes, peeled
225ml/8fl oz/1 cup hot milk
2fl oz/4 tbs extra virgin olive oil
salt and freshly milled black pepper
piece of nutmeg
4–6 black olives, chopped into small pieces

Heat a serving dish.

Bring to the boil in a large pot enough water to completely cover the potatoes and add the salt. Immerse the potatoes, and when the water has returned to the boil, reduce the heat and simmer them until they are soft, about 20 minutes, depending upon their size. Drain them well and return them to the hot pan.

Start mashing them, still over a very low simmer, gradually adding the hot milk and the olive oil. Season well with salt and pepper and a few gratings of nutmeg. Mash again thoroughly and transfer to the serving dish, topped with the chopped black olives.

Deep-fried Courgette (Zucchini) Flowers

It is well worth growing this vegetable for its delicate yellow flowers. Especially prized by Italians, they are highly perishable and command a ridiculously high price in specialist food shops where they can sometimes be bought, individually packaged in cellophane. One of the greatest pleasures of a Mediterranean holiday is a leisurely, early-morning visit to the vegetable markets, selecting squeaky fresh specimens with the tender yellow flowers still attached.

2 tbs pine nuts
2 eggs, beaten
50g/2oz flour
2fl oz/4 tbs water
1 medium onion, diced
3 ripe tomatoes, peeled and diced (or three plum tomatoes
from a can, chopped)
1fl oz/2 tbs olive oil
pinch of oregano
140ml/5fl oz/⅔ cup of dry white wine
110g/4oz cooked rice
salt
freshly milled black pepper
some basil leaves, washed and chopped
75g/3 oz ricotta cheese, crumbled
12 courgette (zucchini) flowers
225ml/8fl oz/1 cup olive oil for frying the flowers

Toast the pine nuts in a dry pan over high heat, until golden.

Prepare the batter by mixing together thoroughly the beaten eggs, flour and water.

Heat 1fl oz/2 tbs of olive oil and simmer the onions until soft. Add the tomatoes, oregano and, a few minutes later, the white wine. Season, cook to a pulp, then stir in the rice. Transfer to a bowl and mix in the pine nuts, basil and ricotta.

Carefully stuff the flowers with the mixture, taking care not to split them.

Heat the cup of olive oil in a non-stick pan until it starts to smoke. Stir the batter, dip the flowers in it and slip them in pairs into the hot oil. Turn once and remove them with a slotted spoon as soon as they are golden, and drain. Serve hot, with a fresh tomato sauce.

A much simpler way of enjoying these delicacies is to coat them in the batter and fry them in olive oil, without a filling.

FISH STEAKS EN PAPILLOTE

An effective and ubiquitous way of cooking filleted or steaks of white-fleshed Mediterranean fish, including red mullet, John Dory, sea bream, snapper, grouper and sea bass (or alternative fish from North Atlantic waters, such as cod, hake, haddock or halibut) is simply to bake them in foil parcels, with herbs, olive oil, a little wine or water, and some vegetables.

1fl oz/2 tbs olive oil for softening the vegetables
1 tbs olive oil for wiping foil
2 cloves of garlic, peeled and chopped
1 large carrot, peeled and diced
8 shallots, peeled and sliced
4 medium potatoes, peeled and very thinly sliced
4 ripe tomatoes, peeled and chopped
800g/1¾lb of any of the above fish
generous handful of fresh parsley, washed and chopped
salt and freshly milled black pepper
110ml/4fl oz/½ cup dry white wine
a little extra virgin olive oil to sprinkle over the fish
1 lemon, cut into quarters

Preheat the oven to 200°C/400°F/gas mark 6. Have ready 4 individual rectangles of foil, large enough to envelope each portion. Wipe each one with olive oil.

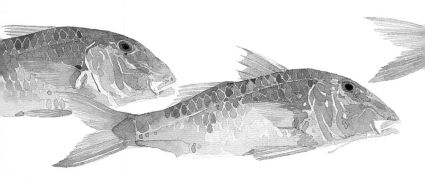

Heat the remaining olive oil in a pan and sauté the garlic, carrot, shallots and potatoes for a minute. Cover, reduce the heat and simmer until soft, stirring once (5 minutes). Add the tomatoes and cook, uncovered, for a further 3 or 4 minutes.

Remove from the heat. Divide the vegetables between the 4 portions, spreading a layer on the oiled foil. Arrange the fish on top, scatter liberally with parsley, season, pour over a little white wine and sprinkle with extra virgin olive oil (2–3 tsp per portion). Fold the parcels over tightly to seal.

Bake until the fish is flaky, 10–20 minutes, depending upon size. Serve, still tightly wrapped, on hot plates, garnished with lemon wedges. Accompany with a salad of dressed leaves or lightly boiled green beans.

Aubergine (Eggplant) Fritters

This vegetable (technically a fruit) is a favourite with Mediterranean cooks. Here is a very simple way of preparing it, perhaps accompanied by alioli and two or three other tapas or *meze* dishes. Unless you are using very large, seedy specimens, the salting process recommended in most cookery books to purge bitter juices is actually unnecessary with today's strains.

> 3 medium or 2 large aubergines (eggplants)
> 225ml/8fl oz/1 cup olive oil
> 175g/6oz/1 cup flour
> salt
> 1 lemon, quartered

Wash the aubergines and dry them. Cut them vertically, then slice each half vertically. Trim off the spongy white flesh from the centre of each quarter, to leave approximately 1cm/½ inch attached to the skin. Now slice the quarters into little segments, each approximately 5cm/2½ inches long, like french fries. Toss them in the flour.

Now heat the oil in a frying pan and when this starts to smoke, put in a batch of segments. Fry until they turn golden and remove with a slotted spoon. Transfer to paper towel and sprinkle with salt. Repeat until all the segments are done. Serve immediately, garnished with lemon quarters.

Preserving in Olive Oil

Italians, Spaniards and French are great preservers of garden and wild produce alike, preferring choice ingredients such as sun-dried tomatoes, baby artichokes and aubergines (eggplants), sweet peppers, and wild mushrooms, especially ceps (king boleti). In Provence, chèvres (little goat's milk cheese,) are also put in oil with wild mountain herbs. You can buy them all ready made, but it is much cheaper and more satisfying to make your own preserves for family and friends.

Chèvres à l'huile

Fill a jar with any variety of soft or medium soft little goat's cheeses (*Crottins de Chavignol* are ideal), adding sprigs of fresh rosemary, marjoram, sage and thyme, a dozen black peppercorns and 2 or 3 dried chillies, and fill the jar with olive oil to cover. Steep for 10 days and consume within a month.

Pomodori secchi sott'olio

Sadly, Britain cannot provide the right conditions of fierce, sustained sunshine to really concentrate the flavour of dried tomatoes, but I imagine that certain American states enjoying Mediterranean or sub-tropical climates probably can. I have never tried drying my own tomatoes, but the theory is simple enough: they are halved, salted and spread out in full sun for a week or so where they will shrivel and turn leathery. The dried tomatoes you buy in specialist food stores and Italian delicatessens are grown in the south of Italy, especially around Naples. Traditionally, each tomato half is stuffed with anchovy, but you can experiment with different combinations of aromatics instead.

Put 225g/8oz dried tomatoes into a bowl with just enough vinegared water to cover (use 1 tbs of wine vinegar for every 225ml/8fl oz/1 cup of water). Leave to soak for at least 2 hours to soften them. Drain thoroughly, put them in a preserving jar and insert any combination of the following: sprigs of fresh thyme, rosemary, marjoram, basil, bay leaves, peeled cloves of garlic, dried fennel seeds, and chillies. Leave for a week or so and serve the halves stuffed with fresh mozzarella and basil to accompany other *antipasti*, or prepare the pesto on page 35. When the tomatoes have all disappeared, strain the oil and use it to flavour cheeses, salads and pasta.

Fungi sott'olio

The author, restaurateur and specialist food retailer Antonio Carluccio has taught many people (not least me) a great deal about finding, identifying, cooking and preserving all manner of wild mushrooms. This definitive recipe is from his book *A Passion for Mushrooms*. Always have your mushrooms checked by an expert, as all poisonous varieties will make you severely ill and a few are deadly.

To sterilize 2 kg/4 lbs of firm young specimens, simmer them for 5–10 minutes (depending on size) in a mixture of 1 litre/2¼ pints of good white wine vinegar, ½ litre/⅘ pint of water, 2 tbs salt, 5 bay leaves and 10 cloves. Drain without touching them with your hands and allow them to cool. Sterilize enough preserving jars to accommodate the mushrooms and put them in with a sterilized spoon, adding a little olive oil and mixing them gently so as to release any trapped air bubbles, and ensure that the oil reaches all parts of the mushrooms. Repeat, top up with olive oil and seal tightly. Keep for at least 1 month before use.

Making Infusions of Olive Oil

Various combinations of fresh and dried herbs and spices will make interesting flavoured oils for dressings and marinades. They are less suitable for cooking as their strong flavours may overwhelm the other ingredients.

Some of these are also available commercially, such as Tuscan lemon and herb oils, fungi oils flavoured with truffles or ceps (porcini, king boletus) and Provençal herb and pimento oils (see page 2 for mail order addresses).

Here are some suggestions for several distinctive oils flavoured with a variety of ingredients. Each can be prepared in a small lidded jar or similar sealed glass container holding 225ml/8fl oz/1 cup of olive oil. Because they have not been sterilized, it is essential to remove fresh ingredients such as herbs after 2 weeks, lest they turn mouldy.

Chilli oil

Wash a dozen fresh red and green chilli peppers, preferably the smaller, hot varieties, then dry them thoroughly and score them all over with the tip of a sharp knife. Put them in a clean, dry bottle filled with olive oil. Leave to infuse for up to 2 weeks. Alternatively, use dried chillies.

Porcini oil

12g/½oz of dried porcini (cep, king boletus) mushrooms will impart a delicious aroma to a small quantity of oil. You can use blended olive oil, but extra virgin is more opulent, as befits the luxury of the flavouring ingredient. When the aroma is unmistakably mushroomy, the oil is ready for use.

Garlic and basil oil

Peel 2 or 3 cloves of garlic and put them and a few sprigs of fresh basil in a jar and fill with extra virgin olive oil. Leave for up to 2 weeks and remove the flavouring ingredients.

Rosemary and bay oil

Steep 2 or 3 fresh sprigs of rosemary and 2 bay leaves in extra virgin olive oil for two weeks, then remove the herbs.

Sun-dried tomato oil

When you have finished the last of your sun-dried tomatoes, prepared following the recipe on page 62, strain the oil in which they were preserved through a sieve and use a few drops to impart a marvellous flavour to cheeses, or to dress a classic *insalata tricolore* of mozzarella, tomato and basil.

Ginger and fennel seed oil

Peel a chunk of fresh ginger about 3cm/1½ inches square and slice thinly. Lightly crush 2 tsp of fennel seeds in a mortar. Steep the spices with olive oil for up to 2 weeks then strain the oil.

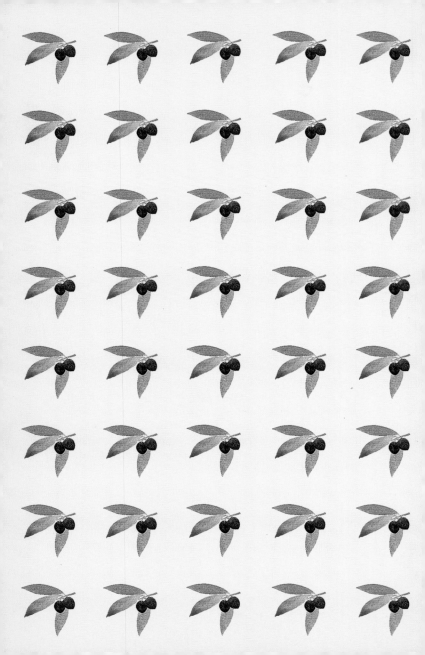